Any Proper Weave

Any Proper Weave

Poems by

Allison Joseph

Cover design by Shay Culligan

ISBN: 978-1-954353-98-5

Kelsay Books
502 South 1040 East, A-119
American Fork, Utah 84003
Kelsaybooks.com

Acknowledgments

Poems from this collection appeared previously in the following journals:

HEArt Online: "Ego Training: Advice for Girls and Women," "Sisterhood Ghazal"

Local News: Poems About Small Towns anthology (ed. Tom Montag and David Graham, MWPH Books): "Ode to an Unloved Town"

Silver of Stone Magazine: "Running While Black"

SWWIM Every Day: "To Answer Verlaine"

TAB: A Journal of Poetry and Poetics: "Compliance"

Contents

Ars Poetica

Poets don't have to vote—it's true;
I read it in the Constitution
and everything I read, the way
I read it, is truth. We don't
have to vote or pay taxes
or parking fines—we live
outside of money, such eager freaks
for envy and pain. When I was young,
I wrote poems so I didn't have
to speak to the large looming
people I lived with—you call
them parents—always with
their yelling and their desire
that I perform these acts they called
"chores"—*I'd rather not,* I'd say
and they'd shove that rag in
my hand or that broom or that
sponge. Who was I to tell them
poets don't clean? Who was I
at all: covert lover of the dictionary,
stealthy pencil hoarder, singer
in so many awkward voices?
Can't you see me back then—
melancholy brace face with a
thousand questions, skinny
in my hand-me-downs,
desperate to be bigger than
I was, mismatched socks
and sad attitude. I know
they wondered what they'd
given birth to—why couldn't I be
a regular brown girl, not this

worried wretch who only
played with words, her dolls,
once worshipped, now neglected
and dusty beneath a twin bed's ruffles?
Who is this, they'd say, and *why is she here?*

Beyond America

God bless all lands that I will never see—
all countries where the language isn't mine,
where people dress so differently than me,
their skin an absent shade of dark, a kind
of sheen that underscores a history
I never read about in school or saw
depicted on TV. God keep them free—
all citizens who challenge foreign laws,
all mothers shaping worlds for progeny,
all workers fighting for a living wage,
all children with the bleakest destinies,
all elderly and prematurely-aged.
God bless the hungry and the hesitant
in every house and town, each resident.

Scar Tissue

I hesitate to touch the skin that's burned—
to feel your palms, once smooth, but now seared rough,
the pain of accidental heat enough
to make me turn away. I've tried to earn
your trust, to show you that I've tried to learn
required tenderness, the sentimental stuff
that comes to those who forfeit being tough,
who live with the emotions that I spurn.
I'm scared to let your scars confront my eyes,
admitting I don't want to see what's there,
repressing what will break me if I let
that moment, full of flame, be realized.
You think that I've gone numb, but I've gone scared.
Your agony's much greater than my sweat.

To Answer Verlaine

What mad Negro, or tone-deaf child
created this penny jewel, this crime,
that rings hollow, false under the file?
           "Ars Poetica," Paul Verlaine

This mad negro has skills
you and all those pasty symbolists
better recognize, music in my
very walk, my laughter like Langston's.
I have my gaudy jewels:
shiny dime store pendants,
cubic zirconia rings,
my sold-on-late-night-television
phony diamond earrings,
and I make them look good—
strutting without a stutter,
striding in my own glistening skin.
My only crime was to be born
in this subtle and shaded hue,
born to marvel at curious things
until I had to write them down
ringing with the very sound of verse,
a kind of molten dignity
even a mad negro could recognize,
even on the edge of sanity—
knife slice of all that enmity,
all those ugly scratches history
etched onto my eyeballs.
Far from false, but still in your files—
a literary suspect, accessible wreck,
baby girl not fit for the Captain's table.
Riddle me this, Verlaine:
how many poets does it take
to stop a war, to broker a peace,

to cut of a piece of any
reader's heart, swallow it whole,
and live? I don't know if you know
how it truly feels to be mad,
angered under the surface
of myriad subtleties while another
campus rages, and a city blisters with gunfire.
I'd like to offer you any one of a dozen
seats, invite you to listen while I
switch my style, silence when I spit it out.

Compliance

after Paul Laurence Dunbar

We wore the mask but we are broken still,
broken bodies drained of joy and skill,
the evidence denied, argued away—
the violence enacted, on display

for anyone to share or like, for thrills.
So many broken bodies stripped of will,
so many useless arguments until
another incident. Then more replays.
We wore the mask,

tried to comply with rules, and still we're spilled—
our blood a simple fetish. Those who kill
will kill again, no matter how we pray,
no matter how we issue our dismay.
The lust for blood is sport. To die is play.
We wore the mask.

After Surfacing

So how are you coping
with all that's gone wrong
indulging and doping
or crafting a song

with all that's gone wrong
why fight for what's right
indulging and hoping
these wrecks will be slight

why fight for what's right
why bother at all
these wrecks will be slight
surviving the fall

why bother at all
why wake up and rise
surviving the fall
means hearing those lies

why wake up and rise
world slaps you back down
and hearing their lies
you know you're not sound

world slaps you back down
when you're on your feet
you know you're not sound
and feel each defeat

when you're on your feet
and flailing about
you feel each defeat
and each stinging doubt

and flailing about
you feel where you break
with each stinging doubt
you harness each ache

you feel where you break
indulging and hoping
you harness each ache
each lesson in coping

Memo from the Accused Girl

the school did not protect me
dismissing my complaint
the school called me a liar
said I should choose my dates

with wisdom and discretion
that I should be demure
that kind of education's
not what I'm paying for

they called me loud and crazy
for speaking up and out
preferring I stay lazy
abhorring how I shout

to make sure that my anger
goes everywhere at once
past all the campus officers
that mostly useless bunch

they came to get my interview
as if it were a joke
an ugly laughing audience
every time I spoke

so I went to the hospital
for them to stitch me up
somehow I was the one to blame—
my hair, my dress, makeup

all made me "someone's slut"
instead of someone's daughter,
somebody's angel child.
again I heard their laughter,

again I heard their blame.
But I won't let my anger
be buried under shame
not silent any longer

when frat boys speak my name.

Things Girls Hear

You should smile more—you'd be
so much prettier if you smiled.
And what's with your hair?
You should straighten it,
then curl it, then brush the curls
so they look natural. And speaking
of natural, you should wear makeup,
just a bit of it—bring out your eyes
more, which are beautiful by the way,
except maybe you should—and I
say this out of love—get those
colored contacts everyone's
talking about. You could try
blue eyes or hazel eyes and
all you'd have to do is put them in
everyday—no trouble at all.
You should definitely dress
a little better—I mean, you've
got a great body—why not show
it off, let people know what
you're working with? You
should wear skirts. Or dresses.
But not those dresses that look
like they're made with little
girls in mind—what are they
called—baby dolls? Yeah,
not for you—they'll just make
you look fat when you aren't,
and that's no good, isn't it?
You should wear heels
sometimes—I mean, if
you're going to wear dresses,

then you shouldn't wear sneakers
with them, unless you are wearing
a suit and just wearing sneakers
before you get to your job.
It's okay then, I suppose.
But if you're going to wear
a dress or a skirt to a bar,
then at least have the decency
to wear a pair of heels,
it looks so much nicer that way,
and you do want to look nice,
don't you? Sure, we all do—
even guys—they just don't know
it yet. And you should really
think about a good bra,
some white strips for those teeth,
some earrings and jewelry—but
no nose stud or belly ring,
and some nail polish, since no one
likes naked hands. You should
be good to go then, and no one
will be able to resist you, you vixen!

Don't Speak to Me

I'll ask you not to brush away my pain
to claim you know my feelings more than me
explaining what I've lived through yet again
debating every nuance that I see

I'll ask you not to argue that I'm wrong
when I have nightmare visions of this land
when I dissect each patriotic song
admitting that this nation's less than grand

for some of us who live in darker skin.
I'll ask you now to stop your blunt attacks
proclaiming I must take it on the chin,
describing all the courage that I lack.

I have a right to all this angry grief—
I'll burn down every stage to get relief.

Ego Training: Advice for Girls and Women

When someone asks too much of you, say no.
When strangers ask for favors, hesitate.
Don't go to places you don't want to go.

Walk tall, head up, eyes front. Keep walking straight
past men who whistle threats at you then smile.
When strangers ask for favors, hesitate,

say you'll get back to them, then wait a while.
Don't slouch or sink into your bones, glide tall
past men who whistle threats at you. Don't smile.

Give what you want to give, but don't give all;
keep part of you intact, untouched, pristine.
Don't slouch or sink into your bones, glide tall,

strut if you like and don't think it's obscene
to like yourself when others call you weak.
Keep part of you intact, untouched, pristine,

but speak your mind, not timid, scared or meek
when someone asks too much of you. Say no.
To like yourself when others call you weak,
don't go to places you don't want to go.

Running While Black

The fact that you unleash your pack
of snarling, angry dogs the moment
I trot by, tank top soaked through,
sweaty shoulders bare, the fact
that this neighborhood at the edge
of the milk factory and trailer park,
is where I shouldn't be caught
occurs to me just as your German
Shepherd lunges—his owner too lazy,
unable or unwilling to leash
this animal's muscled anger.
There are places a woman,
dressed for motion, shouldn't go,
crossings that common sense
and history should keep her from.
Yet my stubborn brown body
wants to go where it wants
to go, foolishly thriving on its
own speed. I know that a flash
of bare legs is signal to some
that I am there for the taking,
to be spat at, mocked, forced
off the road into side ditches,
black puddles. Nobody owns
the road, some fiber in me
foolishly wants to believe.
I tell my friends *I get up*
before the rapists and killers
when they cluck about treadmills
and safe gyms. A woman should
be able to go wherever she wants
without being bruised, hissed at
shouted at: *bounce them tits, girl,*

speed it up! Why then, am I the one
shamefaced and sputtering in rage?
Why am I the one they'll blame
when, days later, my body
surfaces in that roadside trench,
that last chance ditch?

Apologia to My Toes

Who am I to ask this much of you:
blisters and broken toenails, bruises
I savor as signal of daring stamina.
Forgive me the hours and miles
on my feet, blood trapped under skin,
callouses gone stony, rough and hardly
beautiful as I hide you in socks
stained from cuts I let accumulate
like a child counting marbles.
You must think I despise you—
the way I lace you into sneakers,
trap you in strappy sandals, hide you
in winter boots as soon as fall
leaves drop. No beach for you,
my bashed digits, my burdened
servants. How you suffer for my
folly. How you grow old and wizened
with all my demanding steps.
And what do you ever get
for your loyalty and service?
A hasty rub, no better than
what a dog gets. One day,
I know you'll revolt,
grounding me until I pay
attention, baby you with
lotions and new insoles,
a pedicure, a paint job.
That day, you'll make me
sorrier than all my lusty wanderings
have ever made you, and I will cry
for mercy, for tenderness, elevating my legs
so that finally, you'll be above all else.

Ode to an Unloved Town

Tucked at the bottom of this unkempt state,
neglected by the governor's latest silence,
your mansions sit, bleak reminders
of the money once held in back room
bank vaults. Few tourists visit this
heartsore town, black and white turned
back into the segregated South, though this
is Illinois, state of Lincoln's justice,
of wealth and cul-de-sacs, private homes.
Here in Cairo, the last grocery store
has closed for good, the health clinic's
only open one day a week, as if pain
has a mid-week schedule, on time
every time. Every child here wants
to grow up, not return, sailing as soon
as a souped-up car and a license
make it so. People die here for want
of doctors, could lie in the center
of the roads as if wanting to be crushed
but so few trucks rumble their way
through here to the interstate—
no produce for the long chill ahead.
Churches still hold their mighty
doors open though—solace
in the winter, sustenance
in the summer, brick refuges
of hope when prisons make martyrs
of this town's men. Even the liquor
stores have bars on their windows;
even the schoolteachers
are on perpetual strike,
and no one wants to look closely,

as if poverty is catching, a fatal
disease. The one good thing
anyone claims here is barbeque,
but smoke and sauce and meat
can't keep a town alive,
keep a man from finding himself
on the riverbank, deciding
whether or not, at this lowest
point in Illinois, to jump
in where the confluence
of waters turn from blue
to brown, and back again.

Sisterhood Ghazal

Be the woman you're destined to be in this life;
graceful in motion, dancing free in this life.

Buy tickets for any train, bus, plane or cab.
So much to hear, do, think and see in this life.

Speak with body and voice, flowing hands—
you don't always have to agree in this life.

Lay burdens down on altars, by lakes,
places to which you can flee in this life.

Eyes to the heavens, fingers to the sky,
hands up to feel the glee in this life.

All numbers on the scale act shady—
not everyone's size three in this life.

Beads and bracelets, bridges and bayous.
Don't have to be one she in this life.

A book, a pen, a solemn afternoon.
Savor your cups of green tea in this life.

Poems should be courted like a bride.
Get down on one knee in this life.

Come up for air beneath the glamour;
listen for your own plea in this life.

Every taste and flavor, every grain—
so glad you've come to me in this life.

Hymn of Intolerance

I don't want you living near me;
you pray to a different god.
We pray standing; you pray kneeling,
all that you believe is wrong.

You pray to a different god—
all your priests in satin robes.
All that you believe is wrong;
we don't do the things that you do:

all your priests in satin robes,
all your temples full of sin.
We don't do the things that you do—
worshipping the sky and sun.

All your temples full of sin,
all your whirling endlessly,
worshipping the sky and sun,
instead of learning how to live.

All your whirling endlessly
making fools of divine faith
instead of learning how to live
with the proper dignity.

Making fools of divine faith,
you make all the wrong days holy.
With the proper dignity,
we could save you from your fate.

You make all the wrong days holy.
You babble in your sacred tongues.
We could save you from your fate—
all that sin you dwell among.

You babble in those sacred tongues.
We pray standing. You pray kneeling.
We could save you from your fate,
but I don't want you living near me.

Knowledge Is Power

Let me tell you what I know about blackness,
the older white man says to me, smiling graciously.
He's filling me in on me, learned and tactless,

reveling in his grasp of history,
with elegance and wisdom he must share.
The older white man says to me

it's not about your Afro, your thick hair,
Your problems are much bigger than your scalp.
With elegance and wisdom he must share,

he lectures me about the income gap
between blacks and whites, says I must do my part.
Your problems are much bigger than your scalp,

I want to see you tackle with them in art!
He makes me savior, claims I have a gift.
Between blacks and whites, I'll try to do my part,

by tuning out his voice, his words adrift.
He's filling me in on me, learned and tactless.
He makes me savior, claims I have a gift.
Let me tell you what *I* know about: Blackness.

When I Don't Feel Like Praying

Kabbalah, jesus, allah, Buddha, I
Need your sage advice, your
Eternal wisdom. Let me
Engage in some sort of ritual,
Let me kiss some runic stone
Under a swollen moon,
Notorious and needy,
Taut with the urge to speak.
I want to be flush with knowledge,
Livid with electric letters.
You have something I want,
O mystics, something I'd bruise
Under the skin for, prostrate
God in her own kitchen,
Eager to sift and mix
The celestial
Into the regular,
The page my altar.
Ready to grow, to reach
I beseech all available
Gods, no matter how minor,
Hold me in your palms
Til I can I lift my own.

Instead of a Writers' Colony,

I'm thinking purgatory's not so bad
if I get left alone to write and think,
my quietude descending via ink,
my search for peace insistent, no mere fad
that I'll soon tire of. I won't feel sad
to stumble on the edge, live on the brink
between what's right and wrong, not sink
into despair. This vacuum makes me glad—
this emptiness a respite from my fears,
an echo chamber blanked of all I love,
platoon of vacant passages and rooms,
a way station of decades, minutes, years.
If heaven stays unreachable above,
then purgatory's where I'll live and bloom.

Ode to Earplugs

How glorious it is not to hear
the labile screaming baby
in the crowded train car,
the vicious bickering

of that couple behind him,
bliss not to hear the unrelenting
explosions erupting from the movie
on some schoolboy's laptop,

nurturing silence while a gum-
chewing teen mom blathers
into her cell phone about
some dude named Tyrone

who has owed her money
for fifteen months, back child support
she'll never see—since Tyrone or Floyd
or Darryl or whatever his name is

has long since moved out of
town, of state, of cell phone
range. I do not hear these things
because of your round soft yielding grace.

You obliterate decibels
like killing invaders, leave me
headache-free and unremittingly pleasant.
Oh you are awesome indeed,

amazing as you block the madness
that makes me hate humankind—
with you softly couched in my ears,
plugged in just so, I can smile

at that yowling baby, admire
the flush of his red cheeks.
I can admire the movie's cinematography,
silent as another apocalypse

is averted in another superhero movie.
I can smile, offer a fresh piece
of gum to the teen mom,
give her a tissue to wipe

her daughter's snotty nose.
And as for that couple,
tattered and blistered
and talking rough,

it is enough to know
we'll never be them,
that when I squeeze
then slip earplugs in

next to my love at night
all I'm fending off is the sound
of his errant snoring, rumblings
forced upon him to keep him alive.

Woman Waiting

I'm waiting in the airport
for the hour of redemption
heavy baggage for the journey
weighting me at the wrists
        I'm waiting in the train station
        for a minute of consolation
        watching arrivals and departures
        with a tattered schedule
I'm waiting in the supermarket
for a fraction of compassion
briefest eye contact
exchanged for my change
        I'm waiting in the hospital
        for a sliver of insight
        all those numbers on my chart
        some headache I can't read
I'm waiting in the bus depot
for a diagram of empathy
some chart of all the routes
to make a clean escape
        I'm waiting in the alleyway
        for a gram of grace
        some bit of exaltation
        to keep me from my own throat
I'm waiting in the settlement
for a flask of fantasy
some deep draught
I cannot help choke down
        I'm waiting in the bathroom
        for an inch of lucidity
        some scrap of rest
        unknown to any mirror

I'm waiting in the orchard
for a jigger of gratitude
some split of land unfettered
by the bruises of weather
   I'm waiting in the graveyard
   for a flash, a siren, a signal,
   for confirmation this world
   is more than anticipation
   more than this mourning
   collapsing and unraveling
   never adding up
   to any proper weave

About the Author

Allison Joseph lives, writes, and teaches in Carbondale, Illinois, where she is on the faculty of Southern Illinois University Carbondale. She serves as editor and poetry editor of *Crab Orchard Review* and is the founding editor of No Chair Press. Her most recent full-length collections of poetry are *Confessions of a Barefaced Woman* (Red Hen Press) and *Lexicon* (Red Hen Press). She is the widow of the late poet and editor, Jon Tribble.